The Life and Death of

Martin Luther King.

TO MY MOTHER, SISTERS AND BROTHERS

The Life and Death of

Martin Luther King.

Raymond W. Erhijivwo.

AFRIKAN KIN PUBLICATIONS
LONDON

British Library Cataloguing in Publication Data. A catalogue record for this book is available from the British Library.

Printed by Q Print
London

Cover by Steve Lane

AFRIKAN KIN PUBLICATIONS
P. O. BOX 4211
LONDON
SE14 6LP
UK

ISBN - 1 899482 - 008

Preface

People write for many different reasons. This book is Africancentric in its approach and is very much a part of the African America Investigations series. This means that the reader will find ample opportunity to question, argue, disagree and resolve issues that have been raised. It is for this reason and indeed to mark the thirtieth anniversary of King's death that I write. I am also pleased that the publication of this book coincides with the National Year of Reading.

However, this book may not have been possible if I had not received initial support from a number of people. I should like to thank Lewisham Education, in particular, Paul Hann, former English Inspector for Schools, for helping to provide the opportunity for me to research secondary school students.

I should also like to thank Bev Clarke Brown at the Lewisham Professional Development Centre. She initially helped to create opportunities for me and students in the London boroughs to discuss, debate and promote the work of Martin Luther King.

For that part of my research which took me to the USA, I am grateful to Mr Basil Phillips of Johnson Publishing

Company. Also, for the assistance given at The King Center in Atlanta, I am deeply indebted to the then senior librarian, Mr Bruce Keyes. He was very willing to assist me in all my requests for files and he remained ready to discuss any aspect of King's work. I have benefited from that.

I do not forget the contribution of the SCLC office in Atlanta; the Rev. Mr Osburn and many other staff made me welcome amid their preparations and heavy schedule for the thirtieth-anniversary march on Washington. They gave me much of their time. Thank you.

Cesar Rocha and Devon Stewart have been the information technological pilots of this work and I must thank them. Thanks also to Steve Lane for the design of the cover and for his undying optimism and generosity constantly shown. These last two qualities have been demonstrated by many others: Nana Yaa Mensah, Ben Kpogho, Delroy Constantine-Simms, Julie Elizabeth, Pelisa Pama, and former Assistant Director of Education for Haringey, Ms Leela Ramdeen.These people have all helped me to steer the work through the dark clouds that sometimes shadow any work involving lengthy research. They have reminded me why I have chosen to write the book. Much respect is due to them. Nor can I forget Mia

Morris for her work involving motivational speakers and events, and Dr Kimani Nehusi of the University of East London - he provided constructive criticism of my work.

Also, families are important in our lives in so many ways and I am thankful to mine for all the right reasons.

You, the reader, are very important. However you view this book, do remember that the forthcoming titles in the series will address in greater detail many issues that arise in this one; not least, who killed Martin Luther King, Jr., what killed nonviolence, and what became of the black power movement. I hope that you find the book, and especially the series as a whole, challenging and thought-provoking.

Last, but not least, I must thank God for allowing me to complete this work.

RWE

London
January 1998

Abbreviations

ACMHR: Alabama Christian Movement for Human Rights

CCCO: Coordinating Council of Community Organisations

CORE: Congress of Racial Equality

CFM: Chicago Freedom Movement

MIA: Montgomery Improvement Association

MFDP: Mississippi Freedom Democratic Party

NAACP: National Association for the Advancement of Colored People

SCLC: Southern Christian Leadership Conference

SNCC: Student Nonviolent Coordinating Committee

UAW: United Automobile Workers

Contents

In the Beginning

When I was a child, I spake as a child, I
understood as a child, I thought as a
child: but when I became a man I put
away childish things.
1 Corinthians 13

This early lesson from the chapter on love of 1
Corinthians symbolises Martin Luther King, Jr.'s
life and death. It also came to represent an
African-American awakening, the like of which
would not be seen again in twentieth-century
America.

Some features of our past exist over long
periods of time, generations. This is the case of
the African-Americans whose struggles in the
1950s and 1960s in America serve to teach us
many lessons. During this period the concept of
freedom was invested with new meaning, giving
emphasis to another very important concept that
America had merely paid lip service to: equality.
These were concepts central to the whole civil

rights movement in America: from the right to sit down on a bus - like any other American citizen - to the right to vote. This movement began with a woman called Rosa Parks and a man named Martin Luther King, Jr., in Montgomery, Alabama. He was born in Atlanta, Georgia.

As a child, King was much influenced by the church. His father was a Baptist preacher. His mother was a teacher. He was the middle child of three, junior to a sister, Christine, and senior to a brother, Alfred Daniel.

Born into a materially successful family on 15 January 1929, young Martin grew up in Atlanta. Here, indeed all across America, the racial segregation and discrimination strongly resembled South Africa's apartheid system. This had been the way and the life in America for generations.

At this time young Martin was rather like most other boys of his age. One could in no way predict the contribution of the small boy who chirped " One day I'm gonna get me some big words." By the time he had reached fifteen years of age it was very clear that he possessed intelligence - and later still, maturity - well beyond his years.

At fifteen he was admitted to Morehouse College. There he was always well dressed and meticulously groomed. This institution was a learning centre well reputed for its teaching of young African-American men. During his early stages at Morehouse, King flirted with the idea of becoming a medical doctor and later a lawyer. He eventually specialised in sociology and by 1947 - at eighteen - he had settled upon a life in the ministry. He quickly became assistant pastor at his father's church, the Ebenezer Baptist, in Atlanta.

The following year, 1948, saw him ordained as a Baptist minister; it also saw him receive his BA degree in sociology from Morehouse. But King wanted to go on to a seminary - a white seminary. Perhaps the desire to do this was the result of his wishing to prove he was as good as anyone. He was admitted to his chosen seminary, Crozer Theological Seminary, in Pennsylvania. This was 1948, the year in which the US Supreme Court ruled that federal and state courts could not enforce laws which barred people from owning property on the basis of race; this was also the year when President Truman ordered racial integration of all units of the US armed forces.

In 1951 King obtained a degree in divinity from Crozer Seminary and entered Boston University School of Theology to study for a PhD. He would receive his PhD. in systematic theology in June 1955. However, in the coming years King would assume the awesome responsibility of a leader. His readiness to meet the challenges of this leadership would spark an awakening in the South, and later all over America.

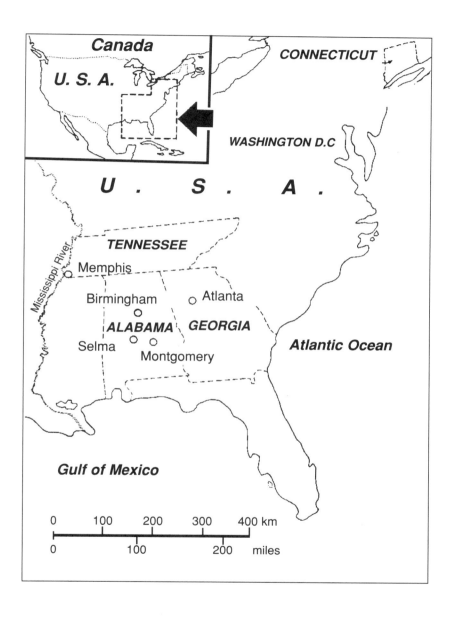

Montgomery

Tired of being trampled over by the iron feet of oppression.

Since his graduation from Crozer, King had wanted to marry. It was early 1952 when Martin Luther King met Coretta Scott. Their first telephone conversations were a combination of directness, humility and humour, and the patient recognition of lyrics. On their first date King learned that Coretta had grown up in rural Alabama and had studied at Antioch College in Ohio. She was currently studying at Boston's New England Conservatory of Music in order to become a classical singer.

The courting continued until 18 June 1953 when the two became husband and wife. At her marriage, Coretta kept her own surname, adding 'King', thereby becoming Mrs Coretta Scott King. They would have four children in their married life together.

In the following year, 1954, King moved to Alabama to take up the post of pastor of Dexter Avenue Baptist Church in Montgomery. Yet 1954 was also the year of a landmark decision by the US Supreme Court; it ruled unanimously in the case of *Brown v. Board of Education of Topeka* that racial segregation in public schools is unconstitutional. This was a particularly significant decision for King because, unbeknown to him, this very same issue - segregation within educational institutions - was what he would help bring to light in the civil rights movement. However, for the time being, it rested in the background of a racially troubled South, of which Montgomery was no exception.

However, in Mississippi, violent terror kept a segregated American South in check with the 'rules' of segregation, purporting that white supremacy was a right not to be questioned. Thus, the taking of Emmett Till's life for 'talking fresh' to a white girl might have been just another murder in Mississippi. Not so, Till's murder sparked a change in personal courage, most evident in Mose Wright, Till's uncle. His personal account of the events that led to Till's murder was both brave and moving to many. The tall, slim man told how a white man had come looking for Till one Sunday morning with a flashlight in one hand and a pistol in the other. This man took Till away. The uncle never saw his nephew alive again. Till's body, so badly damaged it could barely be identified, was found floating in the Tallahatchie River in Mississippi. He was only fourteen. Mose Wright gave evidence in court which clearly identified one of the accused murderers, but to no avail, the implicated Roy Bryant and J. W. Myland were found not guilty.

Another act of personal courage took place in the South in 1955, this time in Montgomery. This act of courage, however, set a trend.

Montgomery was the cradle of the Confederacy: 1861 slave owners in the South had established the Confederate States of America; they had established a provincial government comprising eleven slave states. This was in defiance of

President Abraham Lincoln and led to the American Civil War. It was because of this background that Montgomery was called the cradle of the Confederacy.

Even so, 1 December 1955 was to be a different day in the history of Montgomery. It was on this day that Rosa Parks, a forty-two-year-old African-American woman refused to give up her seat to a white passenger while riding on a Montgomery bus. For this she was arrested. The response to this act of courage was altogether different from Mose Wright's act of courage. This act was thoroughly supported by individuals and African-American organisations within the community. It made a solid case against segregation and it subsequently set an irreversible trend across America: demonstrations, marches, singing, and the demand for the right to equal treatment under the law.

Rosa Parks' arrest drew a sharp response from within the African-American community of Montgomery. By 2 December, preparations for a bus boycott were under way. Leaflets were printed to discourage people from using the buses in protest at Rosa Parks' arrest. People were called to attend a mass meeting on 5 December.

That evening thousands of African-American people attended the meeting. It was agreed that an organisation should be set up and called the Montgomery Improvement Association (MIA) and Martin Luther King, Jr., was to be its president. It was on this evening that he addressed the people, saying:

> There comes a time when people get tired. We are here this evening to say to those who have mistreated us so long that we are tired - tired of being segregated and humiliated, tired of being trampled over by the brutal feet of oppression.

From this evening on, the African-American community of Montgomery united and mobilised their forces. They established a car pool to help their supporters travel - especially now that the Montgomery bus service was being boycotted.

Many walked to work or shared cars with other African-Americans going in the same direction. Their business community worked closely with the church community to ensure a coordinated, effective and well-managed boycott. It continued in this manner for over a year.

It was now 1956 and President Eisenhower had already shown some acknowledgement of civil rights in his public support of the NAACP in the case of *Brown v. Board of Education* - but was this enough? The bus boycott case was going to trial and Montgomery was attracting international media attention. A US federal court order of June 1956 declared the segregated buses in Montgomery unconstitutional. However, lawyers for Montgomery and the State of Alabama appealed this decision to the Supreme Court.This meant the segregation laws remained in effect until the decision of the highest court. Five months later, on 13 November, the Supreme Court declared Alabama's segregated buses unconstitutional; Montgomery's segregated buses were now deemed illegal and King had won an important public victory as leader of the MIA. Later, in the calm reflection of the early stages of the struggle, some would say that "if Rosa Parks hadn't sat down, Martin Luther King never would have stood up, and if Martin Luther King hadn't stood up, Rosa Parks never would have sat down."

The politics and leadership of the MIA were able to prosper as a result of the hard work that had been undertaken years before by the National Association for the Advancement of Colored People (NAACP) and the Urban League. However, they attempted to end segregation through legal means, not through the mass struggle that would soon characterise the civil rights movement.

In the early stages of the Montgomery bus boycott, King had felt that the demands that were being made were relatively moderate; he did not challenge the system that maintained segregation as such. He assumed the demands would be met with little question; he believed privileged whites would give up their privileges on request. This early encounter with Montgomery taught King a very important lesson: "No one gives up his privileges without strong resistance." Indeed, he saw " the underlying purpose of segregation was to oppress and exploit the segregated, not simply to keep them apart." With this lesson now firmly in mind, King would later emphasise America's shameful race record, thereby elevating the moral character of the struggle itself, and, in so doing, King would learn new and equally important lessons. For the time being, the MIA had won an important victory in the South.

Having achieved its main objective of desegregating the buses in Montgomery, the African-American community needed to tackle other issues and so the Southern Christian Leadership Conference (SCLC) was born in February 1957. King was elected president, and Ralph Abernathy, treasurer. The SCLC was concerned with the civil rights of the African-American. It was this organisation that would later dispatch a request to Washington for talks on civil rights. Indeed, the SCLC would, in due course, send a delegation to meet the President of the USA on matters to do with civil rights.

Albany

Truth is on our side.

President Eisenhower did not reply to King's telegram requesting a meeting to discuss civil rights. After all, King was a mere preacher who had caught the nation's attention by boycotting the buses in Montgomery. Indeed, the President had already shown his support in the form of the 1957 proposed voting rights legislation to extend basic citizenship rights to African-Americans.

Although African-Americans could sit anywhere on a bus in Montgomery, knowing that the change of law supported this, what would happen if they attempted to exercise these same rights in other parts of America? Such an issue as this and others that had been raised during the course of the Montgomery bus boycott were already widely discussed, but they seemed to take particular focus in Greensboro, North

Carolina. There, the radical stance taken by students at the North Carolina Agricultural and Technical College needed organisation and direction, even though the students had already staged sit-ins at the segregated Woolworths stores in the city.

The SCLC recognised this need to organise the students and backed a conference to see that this happened. Perhaps it was this that helped provide a springboard for the Student Nonviolent Coordinating Committee (SNCC). Indeed, the SCLC had developed distinct views on the societal circumstances affecting African-Americans and how to address them at that particular stage. By this time, King was certain of the need for an on-going campaign to lead the struggle against segregation and racism in the USA. He was also certain of the need to launch a nationwide campaign to reward businesses through selective buying, and to punish those that chose to remain segregated. He had chosen to adopt a policy of non-violent direct action which would involve the assistance of volunteers. Perhaps this was a reflection of some of King's earlier studies on civil disobedience, including, as many explained it, the teachings of Gandhi.

It would take a trip to Africa to induce the Eisenhower Administration to agree to talks with King. Vice-President Nixon headed the official US delegation to witness the formal transition of The Gold Coast to the country now known as Ghana. Ghana was asserting her independence of British colonial rule. Her first head of state, Kwame Nkrumah, had also invited Martin Luther King and his wife, Coretta, to the occasion. It was here, then, that King met Nixon and they both witnessed Africa's thirst for change. Under these circumstances, Nixon invited King to private talks on civil rights in Washington. King did not decline the invitation.

Later still, the SCLC would declare to both the Republican and Democratic parties the wish to hear them acknowledge many important points on their political platforms. These points included the rejection of segregation, and the declaration that any form of discrimination is unconstitutional. The SCLC suggested that both parties take a clear moral stance against colonialism and racism in all forms, especially in Africa.

The meeting with Vice President Nixon took place on 13 June 1957. There, at the Capitol, King and Abernathy discussed the need for President Eisenhower to come to the South to back the Supreme Court's ruling on desegregation. There was also another matter to do with voting rights. Large numbers of African-Americans were simply excluded from the democratic process of voting. Many were not registered, and in some states such as Mississippi, registrars would make registration difficult and cumbersome so as to hinder it. This was undemocratic, but it was in line with American segregationist politics.

The Civil Rights Act was passed in 1960 - an acknowledgement to the African-American that their voice had been heard. But there were still problems.

The Albany Movement's contribution to civil rights came in 1961. In February of that year, leading members of the African-American community of Albany, Georgia, demanded that public facilities be desegregated. The Ministerial Alliance, the Federation of Women's Clubs, the Negro Voters League, the Criterion Club, and the NAACP and its youth council had come together to form the Albany Movement. In particular the Albany Movement sought the right of bus and rail facilities to be shared by all Americans and not segregated on the basis of skin colour; they also sought the dismissal of all charges against anti-segregation demonstrators, many of whom had been jailed. Negotiations between the local government and the Albany Movement were making no progress.

Within three months of King's return to pastoral duties in Atlanta, he faced arrest and a jail sentence. The charge was demonstrating with students at a shopping complex. This sentence was influenced by another matter: his driving without a Georgia state license since his return to live in Atlanta. The sentence was very real and King prepared himself for the prospect of four months of hard labour. It would require the influence of Senator John F. Kennedy to get him out of jail. This in fact is what happened and King's father, 'Daddy King', praised the Democratic Party in reply. King had spent eight days in jail.

The Democratic Party needed the support of those African-Americans who could vote and it was aware of the SCLC's wish to register African-Americans to vote. The Democratic Party could provide help in the form of the much sought-after grant that was needed by the SCLC to answer the registration expectations of African-American citizens who could not vote.

The SNCC's input was also crucial to voter registration. They sent a group into Mississippi to spearhead a workforce of students to register African-American voters. Voter registration was important to the civil rights movement, and so were equal opportunities in education. Despite the landmark *Brown v. Board of Education* decision in 1954, America's policy in practice remained largely one of 'separate but equal'.

Nevertheless, a certain James Meredith, applied for admission to the University of Mississippi. If his application were to succeed he would become the first African-American to study at 'Ole Miss'. Mississippi politics dictated this an unlikely event, as not a single African-American student attended white schools or colleges at that point in time in Mississippi, Alabama, or South Carolina. But Meredith's application for admission would first have to be considered by the NAACP's Medgar Evers.

Meanwhile, the Albany Movement was concerned about the high proportion of people jailed for their civil rights action; they called in Martin Luther King, Jr., and the SCLC. King's role in Albany began with his address at the Baptist Church. He had been invited by Dr William Anderson, president of the Albany Movement. Here, King was greeted with the singing cries of

21

"Free-dom, free-dom, free-dom": a joyous welcome before the meeting addressed the business of desegregation.

When the meeting did convene, it was confirmed that no settlement had been reached between the city of Albany and its African-American citizens. Demonstrations would continue the next day - an appeal to City Hall - though King would later reflect that discussion with the business community in Albany would have been more beneficial - but it was the marching and the singing that soon became the hallmark of the whole civil rights movement.

The following day, a march on the courthouse in Albany took place. It was the movement's First Amendment right to picket downtown Albany, but during the march, King, Abernathy and hundreds of others were arrested. King then invited others to join him in jail, saying that, if convicted, he would not pay the fine. Meanwhile, an oral agreement was being reached between the city officials, which included Albany's Mayor Kelly, and the leaders of the Albany Movement. This 'gentlemen's agreement' meant that none of the demonstrators would be brought to trial and there was to be a future meeting with the city commission; but city officials refused to commit themselves to a written agreement; King's $400 security bond was signed, and he and several hundred other demonstrators were released from jail. He returned to Atlanta.

It soon became apparent that the city officials of Albany had no intention of meeting with the Albany Movement leaders, as prearranged meeting after meeting was deferred. It was now January 1962 and still no biracial committee had been established to deal with the problems the protesters faced. So the boycott of the city's buses and white stores continued throughout February, March, April, May, June and July, when King and Abernathy returned to Albany to stand trial for their December arrest. They were sentenced to forty-five days in jail or a $178 fine. They chose jail.

Within two days of their imprisonment they were out of jail; their fines had been paid and nobody seemed to know who had paid them. This was a ploy to get King out of jail. King was not happy about the "subtle and conniving tactics" used to get them out of jail against their will. However, Mayor Kelly and Albany's chief of police, Laurie Pritchett, knew that King's imprisonment would bring a new wave of demonstrations to Albany. This would attract nationwide attention, and while King knew and welcomed all this, Pritchett could not share these sentiments. His arrangement for a secret payment of the fine served to toss King out of jail and avert increased news attention.

King would return again to Albany that same July, once again in search of a way to talk face-to-face with the City Commission. Only on the understanding that negotiations would take place in his absence did he return to Atlanta. However, the Commission did not recognise King as a responsible spokesperson for the African-American citizenry of Albany, and they invited "law-abiding citizens" to attend its meetings. This was indication that nothing had changed as a result of King's departure. Albany was still segregated and some argued that little had been achieved by the tactics of marching, followed by arrest, and bail. However, it taught two crucial lessons that the SCLC would use in their future pitched battle in Birmingham, Alabama.

The first lesson was that the Albany Movement had focused on the evil of segregation - it had not focused on a particular aspect of racial segregation and attempt to win a victory there before moving on to other aspects of desegregation. The second lesson followed from the first: the movement would have had greater success if it had initially targeted and negotiated with Albany's business leaders, rather than the city's elected officials. The demonstrations and marches had not been combined with the boycott of Albany's downtown white stores. The movement's political bargaining power should have come with its ability to influence the city's economic power structure through the boycotting of downtown stores.

Yet all was not lost in the African-Americans' struggle against segregation; truth was on their side.

Birmingham

Great baseball players don't strike themselves out - you've got to put them out.

With great baseball players, one rule remained constant: they never voluntarily give up the opportunity to score. This lesson had to be applied by African-Americans in Birmingham, Alabama: to desegregate that city they had to put racial segregation out of business. Could they really meet this challenge in 1963 America?

James Meredith's application for admission to the University of Mississippi was important for the civil rights movement. It would become a test case for the desegregation of educational institutions across America. With the guidance and advice of Medgar Evers, Meredith would be admitted to the University of Mississippi, much to the annoyance of many of its students. Yet

Mississippi was the home of the white Citizens' Council, formed specifically to crush any kind of racial integration. It was one of the most militant segregationist states in America. Here, in Oxford, Meredith would arrive to register for his classes in late September 1962.

It would take Meredith more than three attempts before he could finally register. The Mississippi National Guard and federal troops would be ordered by President Kennedy to quell the riot that ensued on the October night of his actual registration. More than twenty thousand soldiers stood ready to defend him. This was America, 1962.

Meredith did receive his degree but his case would stand as a poignant reminder to all Americans that racial segregation and discrimination permeated American institutions of higher education.

However, Birmingham, Alabama also had its share of problems the same time that Albany was undergoing its own. Birmingham, 'America's Johannesburg', was a white supremacist city; it had attracted national attention for its strict segregation and racial hatred. Indeed, the governor of Alabama, George Wallace, became the very symbol of resistance to any attempts at racial integration. In January, 1963 he made his stance crystal clear: "I draw the line in the dust and toss the gauntlet before the feet of tyranny and I say segregation now, segregation tomorrow, and segregation forever." It was in this same year that African-American leaders focused on a city within that very state for a major confrontation, Birmingham.

Birmingham was the largest industrial city in the South and Eugene 'Bull' Connor was its Commissioner of Public Safety. He would stand for mayor in Birmingham in the year of 1962, only to be defeated by Albert Boutwell, but Boutwell too was a segregationist. Despite his failure to become mayor, Connor insisted that he could not legally be removed from office until 1965. This meant settling the matter in court. In the meantime he refused to move out of the City Hall offices. This meant that there were, in effect, two governments running Birmingham. However, the matter of desegregation of interstate travel was within federal jurisdiction, and any challenge of this by the city of Birmingham would lead to a confrontation with Washington. Desegregation of restrooms and the upgrading and hiring of African-Americans in the industrial community in Birmingham were also matters that concerned many of its African-American citizens. The SCLC would come to deal with all this. Birmingham had reached a crossroads.

To look after many of their requirements, Birmingham's African-Americans had their own organisations like the Alabama Christian Movement for Human Rights (ACMHR), formed in 1956. It had leaders as Reverends Gardener and Shuttlesworth. In 1963, however, the SCLC decided to support the ACMHR by holding a plenary conference in Birmingham.

Efforts to desegregate the city did not appear to

be working until the Rev. Fred Shuttlesworth advised King that if he came to Birmingham to assist in their struggle, the whole civil rights movement after the experience in Albany, could not only gain prestige, but could also win a victory.

The SCLC decided to make Birmingham the focus of its efforts. It had been agreed that Project C ('C' for confrontation) would be launched in March 1963. It was agreed by the SCLC that the campaign would largely focus upon Birmingham's business community and that they should use lessons from the Albany experience.

King instructed the SCLC headquarters in Atlanta to write confidential letters to the major civil rights organisations: the NAACP, the CORE, the SNCC, and the Southern Regional Council, fully explaining Project C and asking for their cooperation. The religious leaders who assisted at Albany were also informed. In accordance with the whole operation, the

Birmingham Manifesto read as an indication of wrongs that its African-American citizens had encountered:

The patience of an oppressed people can not endure forever . . . . Under the leadership of the Alabama Christian Movement for Human Rights we sought relief by petition for the appeal of the city ordinances requiring segregation and the institution of a merit-hiring policy in city employment.

By the end of the first three days of the Birmingham campaign, there had been a number of lunch-counter sit-ins. The demonstrators had been screened and trained to respond nonviolently to the hostility they were expected to face. These demonstrators would walk to City Hall and be arrested. This was part of the movement's tactics, to fill the jails. However, they did find that the courts were using injunctions to obstruct and eventually crush the direct action tactics of the movement. This denied them their right to peaceable assembly.

On 10 April 1963, the city of Birmingham

obtained a court injunction suspending the marchers' right to demonstrate. A defiant King decided he would disobey this and go to jail for marching. Putting on his working clothes he left the Gaston Motel with Ralph Abernathy and went to the Zion Hall Church where there was a scheduled meeting. From there they marched and many others joined in. They marched and marched until eventually they were arrested. Their arrest was to precede the writing of a famous address: 'Letter from Birmingham Jail'. The letter was, perhaps, most of all a response to the view of eight white Birmingham clergymen who had issued 'An Appeal for Law and Order and Common Sense' while King was in jail; it suggested that a solution of racial problems be sought through the local and federal courts. Yet the federal courts had largely upheld and perpetuated the segregation laws.

In his letter King informed his critics of what steps had been taken to assess the situation in Birmingham before direct action was taken. He then addressed the matter of why African-

Americans could no longer wait.

Perhaps it is easy for those of you who have never felt the stinging darts of segregation to say "Wait". But when you have seen vicious mobs lynch your mothers and fathers at will and drown your sisters and brothers at whim . . . when you suddenly find your tongue twisted and your speech stammering as you seek to explain to your six-year-old daughter why she can't go to the public amusement park that has just been advertised on television . . . when you are harried by day and haunted by night by the fact that you are a Negro . . . then you will understand why we find it difficult to wait.

He continued:

Oppressed people cannot remain oppressed forever . . . . We will win our freedom because the sacred heritage of our nation and the eternal will of God are embodied in our echoing demands.

King's arrest did not stop the plans already established for Birmingham: 'D-day' had yet to be played out. His release from jail after eight days would afford him time to prepare. Thousands of children were used to further the aims of the struggle to have African-Americans recognised as citizens. These young people from the Birmingham community came from colleges and high schools in the area. James Bevel, Dorothy Cotton and Andrew Young had invited them to attend after-school meetings at the churches. Ten-to-the-dozen, they came for training sessions on disciplined civil-disobedience tactics. They had found a great sense of purpose which would need to survive the lifetime of King. This test had yet to come.

They marched, were arrested, and soon began to fill the jails. In an attempt to stop the march of D-day, 'Bull' Connor ordered that water hoses with one hundred pounds of water pressure per square inch be turned on these young demonstrators. This action shocked the general public as national news media reported the events.

Newspapers showed pictures of women lying

prostrate and policemen bending over them with raised clubs. They also showed police dogs' teeth penetrating the flesh of nonviolent marching demonstrators. This was Birmingham, May 1963.

Meanwhile, the economic power structure of Birmingham was bending under the pressure of the boycott of its white downtown stores. The direct action tactics were being used in conjunction with the boycott to force the Birmingham city officials to negotiate with the movement on four key matters: (1) the desegregation of lunch counters and restrooms; (2) the upgrading and hiring of African-Americans on a non-discriminatory basis throughout the industrial and business community in Birmingham; (3) the dropping of charges and the release of jailed demonstrators; (4) the creation of a biracial committee to work out a timetable for desegregation in other areas of the city. Agreement was reached on 10 May, 1963, thirty-eight days after Project C had started. The SCLC had won a victory. King and the SCLC left Birmingham.

The Ku Klux Klan, however, were not happy about this agreement, arguing that such a deal was invalid. The bombing of the Gaston Motel, where King had been staying while in Birmingham lead to a large crowd. A confrontation between the police and the crowd followed, resulting in a riot. The racial tension in Birmingham had so intensified since Project C that on 11 June, 1963, President Kennedy was obliged to make the following statement:

> The events in Birmingham and elsewhere have so increased the cries for equality that no city or state or legislative body can truthfully choose to ignore them. The fires of frustration and discord are burning in every city . . . . Next week I shall ask the Congress of the United States to act, to make a commitment it has not fully made this century to the proposition that race has no place in American life or law.

Meanwhile, Kennedy had ordered three thousand federal troops to position themselves near Birmingham, while he remained poised to federalise the Alabama National Guard.

Later, in September, would come the murder by bombing of four girls at the Sixteenth Street Baptist Church in Birmingham. The violent rage that followed in the streets of Birmingham would not bring them back to life, and the chorus at their funeral sang : " W e - e - shall - o - ver - come, some d - a - a - a - a - a - y . . ." - but when? And how?

Plans were already being made for a mass march on Washington. The civil rights leaders were preparing to mobilise the whole of the USA to demonstrate for jobs and freedom.

The Dream and Washington, DC

One Hundred Years Later. . .

It was the success of Birmingham that germinated the seed for the March on Washington. This would be one of America's largest demonstrations. It would be held in the nation's capital city and attract the attention of the whole world. Its main aim was to press President Kennedy to sign an executive order against racial segregation.

Asa Philip Randolph's proposal was to send a delegation to Washington to demand the enactment of fair employment legislation and to call for an increased minimum wage to be extended to areas of agriculture and commerce. The SNCC, the CORE and the SCLC responded favourably to this request. These organisations along with several others would be involved in the dramatisation of the political and economic situation that faced African-Americans. The date set for the March on Washington was 28 August 1963.

The main speakers on the day of the march included Asa Randolph of the American Labor Council. In his bud-booming voice he spoke the opening words and presented the following speakers: the Rev. Eugene Carson Blake of the National Council of Churches, John Lewis of the SNCC, Walter Reuther of the United Automobile Workers (UAW), Floyd McKissick of CORE, Roy Wilkins of the NAACP, and Martin Luther King, Jr., of the SCLC.

Asa Philip Randolph's opening address set the tone of what was to come. He spoke of the need for a comprehensive civil rights law which would include guarantees of access to public accommodation for African-Americans, integrated education, protection of voting rights, and a Fair Employment Practices Act to stop job discrimination and bring about a national minimum wage. There was also a need for a federal programme to train and place unemployed workers in jobs, and bar companies guilty of discrimination from federal funds.

It was King's speech, however, that captured the nation's attention. He was the keynote speaker and Randolph described him as "the moral leader" of the nation and "a great dedicated man, a philosopher of the nonviolent system of social behaviour."

Applause greeted the introduction of King and his appearance at the microphone. Placards and handkerchiefs waved and he waited for the chanting to die down. His starting reference point was:

> Five score years ago, a great American . . . signed the Emancipation Proclamation. This momentous decree was a great beacon light of hope to millions of Negro slaves . . .

Here King was reminding America that, in 1863,

President Abraham Lincoln had signed the Emancipation Proclamation: this manifesto declared slaves free from 1 January of that year. King saw this as a "promissory note, to which every American was to fall heir", guaranteeing them the right to life, liberty and the pursuit of happiness. However, 1963 marked one hundred years since the Proclamation should have taken effect: many of the promises of the Proclamation had not been fully kept for African-Americans. Thus, the rights which should have been granted in 1863 to African-Americans became the major cause of the March on Washington in 1963.

King continued in slow monotone: "But one hundred years later, the Negro is still not free." He would repeat the "one hundred years later", more than three times, to emphasise how the life of African-Americans had been crippled by poverty and "exile". This portrayal of their conditions was only the beginning. As he raised the intensity of his message, he cautioned:

It would be fatal for the nation to overlook the

urgency of the moment . . . . There will neither be rest nor tranquillity in America until the Negro is granted his citizenship rights. The whirlwinds of revolt will continue to shake the foundations of our nation until the bright day of justice emerges.

This sharp message to Congress was then followed by a plea to African-Americans:

But there is something that I must say to my people . . . . Let us not seek to satisfy our thirst for freedom by drinking from the cup of bitterness and hatred. We must forever conduct our struggle on the high plane of dignity and discipline.

This was testimony to King's oratorical skills: adjusting his tone while mixing command and commendation; speaking to different groups of his audience, all within the space of a few breaths, as he lowered and raised the tone of his voice. By now he had moved from the short trumpet blasts of oratory to longer, drawn-out passages, "I have a dream today," stretching the word "dr - e - e - e - am," until he reached the climax:

When we allow freedom to ring, when we let it ring from every village and hamlet, from every state and city, we will be able to speed up that day when all of God's children - black men and white men, Jews and Gentiles, Protestants and Catholics - will be able to join hands and sing to the words of the old Negro spiritual, "Free at last, free at last; thank God Almighty, we are free at last."

Tumultuous applause thanked him. This was King at the pinnacle of his career. Nobody knew then that thirty years later, in August 1993, another March on Washington would take place. For now, many praised the march as a great success, but it had been carefully choreographed. For example, the SNCC's John Lewis had wanted to comment to the nation and the world on President Kennedy's proposed civil rights bill:

In good conscience we cannot support the administration's civil rights bill, for it is too little, too late.

He would have continued:

> There's not one thing in the bill that will protect our people from police brutality.

However, he did not say this. Such a criticism might have prevented the nation from hearing the keynote speaker, Martin Luther King, Jr. Lewis would have wanted to ask - but again he did not ask - what was in the bill to ensure the equality of a maid's income with that of her employer; instead, he asked a different rhetorical question:

> Where is the party that will make it unnecessary for us to march on Washington?

To some, the answer would come with the rejection of mainstream American political parties and the formation of the militant Black Panther Movement; to others, the answer would lie in the formation of the Mississippi Freedom Democratic Party (MFDP).

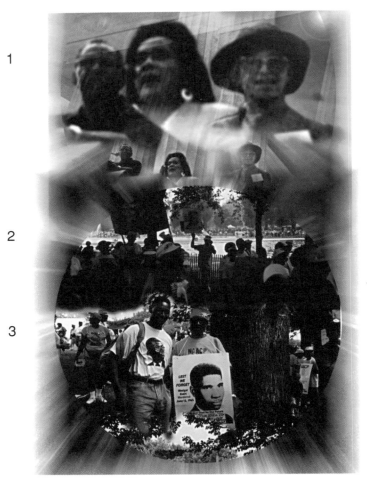

1 L-R: Joseph Lowery, Coretta Scott King and Rosa Parks at the thirtieth-anniversary march on Washington, 1993.

2 By the reflection pool near the Lincoln Memorial they march and remember history.

3 Many pause to rest on their journey to the Lincoln Memorial, 28 August 1993. One marcher (L) wears a T-shirt with face of M.L.King; another (R) holds a poster with the face of Jackson, Mississippi, NAACP leader, Medgar Evers, assassinated 12 June 1963. Many died, few are remembered.

From within the African-American community of Atlanta, a leader of leaders is born. Martin Luther King's birthplace is now an historic site, 501 Auburn Avenue, Atlanta, Georgia.

At the thirtieth-anniversary march, amidst the tens of thousands gathered, a banner rests with the face of Martin Luther King displayed. How long?

And still they march.

Selma

How long? Not long.

President Kennedy had been shot and killed in Dallas, Texas, in November 1963; a twenty-two-year-old Cassius Clay (later known as Muhammad Ali) shocked the boxing world by winning the world heavyweight championship from Sonny Liston, and Congress passed the Civil Rights Act in 1964.

The Civil Rights Act forbade racial discrimination in most public facilities. However, some SNCC members were becoming disillusioned with the government's attempts to help them register voters in Mississippi. Quite apart from the continual arrests the SNCC members experienced in pursuing this objective, the Democratic Party in Mississippi was a segregated party. These circumstances under which they laboured forced the SNCC to change. In one respect the SNCC would retain its role as the student organisation of the SCLC, but it would also develop a new militant stand against racial segregation.

This new militancy was clearly borne out in its formation of the non-segregationist party, the MFDP. This party sought to allow all Mississippians the right to vote; it was a response to Mississippi's segregated Democratic Party. Eventually, it would have some 80,000 registered voters and it would send a delegation to the Democratic Party Convention in Atlantic City, New Jersey, in August 1964.

Yet this last measure was an obstruction of the Democratic Party's main objective of defeating the Republican Party at the next presidential election. The MFDP would not be allowed to represent Mississippi - the Mississippi Democratic Party would do that - it would be allowed only two seats at the convention.

America watched the nationally televised convention, and while a disappointed MFPD considered the offer made to them by the convention's credentials committee, Fanny Lou Hamer, Vice-Chair of the MFDP, broke into song. " Go- o-o, tell it on the moun - tain, over the hills and every-whe-e-re. Go, tell it on the moun-tain - to let my people go-o." Others of the sixty-eight member delegation joined in; they would reject the offer made to them and leave the convention disillusioned. For Fanny Lou Hamer had already put the question to the convention: "Is this America, 'the land of the free and the home of the brave'?" It was America, but American politics had no place for such a party as the MFDP.

On 10 December 1964, Dr Martin Luther King, Jr., was awarded the Nobel Peace Prize. His response was as follows:

> I could not consider the Nobel Peace Prize as an award to me personally. The Nobel Peace Prize is an award to the whole civil rights movement of the United States and to its dedicated leaders.

Despite this acknowledgement on the part of the

international community towards the work of the civil rights movement, there was still a great deal of work to be done. Selma was the next major challenge for Dr King and the civil rights movement.

Selma, Alabama, lying some fifty miles west of Montgomery, would be the last testing ground for the SCLC in the South before its campaign in the northern state of Illinois. Selma was scheduled to be the place for the final push to end the barriers to voter registration. However, the governor of Alabama, George Wallace, had refused to acknowledge African-Americans' right to vote there.

The tactics used for Selma would involve King's imprisonment. This would attract media attention to those very issues that the campaigners wished to raise.

Then, on 2 February 1965, more than two hundred volunteers, marched for the right to vote. They were arrested before they could travel very far past Brown Chapel where they had congregated. Whilst in jail, King sent word to other members of the SCLC that pressure should be brought on the Selma authorities to allow voters more days for their registration. The process of registration had become very slow, and some saw this as an obstacle designed to deny the opportunity to vote to the many African-Americans who had joined the SCLC push in Selma for voter registration. King also asked for a congressional delegation to visit Selma and appear at one of the mass meetings. That was not all; a press conference should be called and some form of activity pursued to keep the cause fresh in the memory of the public; celebrity support should also be sought - this would increase the morale of the demonstrators and show that they had support outside Selma. These carefully planned tactics provoked a response from President Johnson:

All Americans should be indignant when one American is denied the right to vote. The loss of that right to a single citizen undermines the freedom of every citizen.

As if unaware that America had long perpetuated this glaring anomaly, President Johnson was now endorsing the marchers' right to seek the vote. However, a crisis was beginning to arise as King left jail and continued with the planning for the Selma campaign. A rally held by the SCLC's CT. Vivian provided new impetus to the SCLC's plans. This rally at Perry County Courthouse ended in a show of police brutality on nonviolent demonstrators after they had been asked to turn their procession around. In the confusion that followed, a young African-American, Jimmie Lee Jackson, was shot by an Alabama state trooper. He later died.

A symbolic march took place on 7 March to mark the Jackson shooting. However, the plans to march along Highway 80 toward Montgomery were complicated by threats of shooting and bombing. Governor of Alabama, George Wallace, issued an order to stop the marchers; he set the limit of the march at Pettus Bridge.

Meanwhile, more than five hundred marchers

set out on that day. John Lewis of the SNCC and Hosea Williams led this march from Brown Chapel Africa Methodist Church, Selma, to Montgomery. Martin Luther King and Ralph Abernathy returned to Atlanta to perform their pastoral duties in their respective congregations. They did not know until later that the marchers had been stopped at Pettus Bridge in Selma, and that tear gas, charging horses, cattle prods, and clubs had been used by the state troopers to disperse them and drive them back across the bridge. Many had been hurt, some seriously. This action by the Alabama state troopers curtailed their march to Montgomery.

A march planned for 9 March would commence in response to the ill-treatment of these marchers. Again, the marchers did not cross Pettus Bridge, but they were not beaten either. However, it was the march of 21 March that allowed King and others to address the issue of Selma's segregation and discrimination in voter registration. It also allowed time for reflection on the murder of Jimmie Lee Jackson.

This march was bigger than the previous one. It commenced at 1 p.m. and it went according to plan, without any major mishaps. By the third day, the marchers had reached the mid-point of their journey, some thirty miles from Selma. By the end of the fourth day, there were many African-American celebrities present: the legendary Ella Fitzgerald; soul singer, Nina Simone; heavyweight boxing champion, Floyd Patterson; rib-tickling comedian Dick Gregory, and top actor Harry Belafonte. Indeed, it was King's aim to "transform Alabama, the heart of Dixie, into a state with a heart of brotherhood and peace and goodwill."

The next day more than 25,000 people walked the last few miles into Montgomery to Alabama's State capitol building where King gave his response to the treatment of 7 March 1965 on Pettus Bridge:

Our whole campaign in Alabama has been centred around the right to vote. . . . I know some of you are asking today, "How long will it take?". . .

How long? Not long, because no lie can live forever. How long? Not long, because you still reap what you sow. How long? Not long. Because the arm of the moral universe is long, but it bends towards justice. How long? Not long, 'cause mine eyes have seen the glory of the coming of the Lord . . .

The movement had started ten years ago in Montgomery; then, its supporters could clearly be identified as African-American, now it had come home with wide support from a cross-section of the American population.

Later in that month of March, King called for a nationwide boycott of Alabama products until the passage of the voting law allowing African-Americans the right to vote. On 6 August 1965, the Voting Rights Bill became law.

Chicago

Umgowa.

The Voting Rights Act of 1965 allowed federal examiners to supersede local officials in the registration of African-American voters in certain circumstances. Mobutu Sese Seko took power in the Congo. El-Hajj Malik El-Shabazz (Malcolm X) died in a volley of bullets. This was 1965.

After the passage of the voting law, King and the SCLC decided to focus more acutely on other areas like the northern states and the poverty that prevailed in the lives of so many people there.

To address the poverty issue of America would require not merely the tempering of the American economic structure, but large programmes that would restructure American society to bring about a more equal distribution of wealth. But this would bring King into conflict with long-established American patterns of thought and behaviour. This approach would require a different Martin Luther King, Jr., to the one of Montgomery ten years earlier.

Chicago in Illinois, was America's second largest city and was to be used to determine whether the SCLC could succeed in bringing social change to the northern states.

To challenge the issue of poverty in Chicago, the SCLC worked closely with Chicago's Coordinating Council of Community Organisations (CCCO), and together they formed the Chicago Freedom Movement (CFM).

The project concentrated on jobs and housing. The plan was to spend a year in Chicago working with existing organisations, after which the SCLC would remain 'on call'. Thus, the CFM's main objective was to eliminate the ghettos in Chicago. To do this, three steps would have to be taken. First of all the citizens of Chicago would have to be informed of the programme through tenant organisations. Then would come the exposure of Mayor Daley's political machine which was thought to lock many African-Americans into a system of paying high rents while receiving poor standards of service, and being excluded from some of the most prestigious jobs in the city. This helped to foster a cycle of poverty within this community. The last step of the strategy was to create a collective consciousness among the residents, such that there might be a direct confrontation between the existing social structure of Chicago and the new force of the CFM.

King moved into a rehabilitated slum flat with Coretta in January 1966. It was a four-room, $190 a month flat, 1550 South Hamlin Avenue, in the centre of the Lawndale ghetto of Chicago. The lease was signed without the landlord's knowledge that King would be residing there. This would allow him the opportunity to experience the poor conditions that the tenants faced daily.

King's response to the poor housing conditions that many Chicago inhabitants faced was to announce rent strikes. Mayor Daley replied by announcing new programmes to improve the housing conditions of the residents. In effect this served to nullify the SCLC's 'war on slums' initiative. However, the challenge still remained. The CFM was set on organising the people of Chicago into permanent unions for united long term action rather than on a short-term basis for demonstrations and marches only. With permanent unions established, structures could be designed through which the work initiated could be continued. It was this coordinated effort that prompted President Johnson to introduce a new civil rights bill banning discrimination in the sale or rental of housing. The bill would be passed in 1968.

Before then, the CFM worked hard to organise residents into tenant organisations while poor housing conditions were exposed by news coverage. Yet, equally important, was the matter of the economic advancement of African-

Americans in Chicago. If they were to escape the poverty cycle they would need to increase their income. Jesse Jackson was a young SCLC member; his management of Operation Breadbasket seemed to be the answer.

The seeds of Operation Breadbasket had been planted some four years ago and had made some headway in Atlanta already. It was now 1966 and Operation Breadbasket in Chicago was preparing itself for jobs from soft drinks firms and grocery chains. The aim was to increase the income of the African-American community by some $50 million.

In June, 1966 the CFM felt impelled to demonstrate the large-scale activities needed, to prick the conscience of the inhabitants still further, while seeking at the same time a direct confrontation with the power structure that perpetuated the poverty. A planned rally at Soldier Field was intended to answer this call in part, while demonstrations in all-white residential areas of Chicago would address the rest.

Amid the concerns for economic betterment of African-Americans in Chicago and provision of improved affordable housing, King was concerned about the war in Vietnam. America's involvement in this war had caused him to speak out. With the backing of the SCLC, he would later argue that America's war effort in Vietnam was causing great financial problems for its own domestic anti-poverty programme and that a prompt withdrawal from the war should be sought. Long before it was a popular view, King demanded that America's involvement in this war should cease. It was a war America could not win.

Meanwhile, James Meredith was planning a walk of over two hundred miles, from Memphis, Tennessee, to Jackson, Mississippi. Its purpose: to demonstrate that African-Americans could move freely throughout the South without fear of violence. This fear haunted people in this region to the extent that many were afraid to show themselves in order to vote. Meredith's walk started on 5 June 1966.

On 6 June, just before reaching the Mississippi state line on US Highway 51, Meredith was shot and wounded from ambush. This shooting prompted the whole civil rights movement to rethink its course of action for that summer. By coordinated effort on the next day, members of the SNCC and the SCLC marched along the very same highway. This was a very brave act and yet it was crucial if the movement was to reinforce the point that Meredith had been attempting to make in his walk. To capitalise further on their presence in the South, the SCLC decided after three days of marching, to emphasise the importance of voter registration.

They marched into neighbouring communities, encouraging voter registration. This time the marchers were a cross-section of African-Americans and white Americans. This was a tactic by the movement organisers to try to counter the increasing expressions of black nationalism which threatened to challenge the nonviolent approach that King had preached for more than ten years. Until this point nonviolence had been quite effective, but now there was increasing pressure, particularly from the SNCC, for the SCLC to adopt a more militant approach.

And so they marched, black and white together, into the neighbouring communities of Grenada and later Greenwood in Mississippi. It was out of the mobilisation of the march through Lowndes County in Alabama in 1965 that the SNCC found the support to organise itself on a more militant model than that of the SCLC. This new militancy found its voice in Greenwood, where the young SNCC president, Stokely Carmichael, voiced this frustration, filling the ebony night with cries of "black power." A chant would soon characterise this new expression: "Umgowa, black power, peep-peep, bang-bang."

King would ultimately come to terms with the fact that the 'black power' cry was not merely voiced from the anger and despair of a vibrant organisation growing out of the SCLC; he would realise that it was a banner for the ideas that surfaced from the circles of the civil rights movement. The black power cry forced many in the movement to come to terms with the fact that the movement's destiny was ultimately tied up with its history, and that to attempt to seek civil rights gains without first dealing with the matter of identity - 'Africanself' - would not take the movement forward.

Thus, the 'Umgowa' chant would later shape the politics of the civil rights movement in a profound and lasting manner. It would encourage black pride, black enterprise and appreciation of the African heritage. Yet at the time, it was a small thorn in the side of a movement which looked out far and yonder for the broader appeal of the American public.

Back in Chicago, the CFM was planning to hold a rally at Soldier Field, to raise, once again, an awareness of some of Chicago's problems. On 10 July, 1966 the rally took place; in their thousands, demonstrators marched to City Hall, where King made eight demands of the Chicago administration and attached them to the door in the manner of his sixteenth-century namesake, Martin Luther.

The demands were that real-estate agents (1) should refuse to handle property not available to all races. This was coupled by a pledge from banks and loan associations not to discriminate against African-Americans. In addition, (2) the construction of housing should take place outside the ghetto while (3) the city was required to purchase from firms with full-employment policies. Businesses and local government should (4) publish racial employment statistics. There were also demands for: (5) recognition by the county public aid department of unionised welfare recipients, (6) the establishment of a review board of the police department, (7) an immediate desegregation plan in Chicago and (8) the boycotting of discriminatory businesses.

These demands met only with the recommendation that the CFM should encourage the formation of nonprofit construction and rehabilitation corporations. The movement shifted its focus. They would now march into the white neighbourhoods that excluded African-Americans through real-estate agents' unwillingness to sell or rent them property and through the hostility of the residents.

In August 1966, King announced his intention to march to Cicero. This quickly brought the Chicago city administration to the negotiation table. Cicero was symbolic of suburban white American exclusivity. Many organisations stood ready for the march to Cicero: the SCLC, the CORE, the SNCC, the CCCO and many local youth groups. However, two days before the march was due to commence, an agreement was reached with the Chicago administration and the business community. A ten-point plan was accepted by King. This was the Summit Agreement and it called for real-estate agents to post a summary of the city's policy on open housing. Housing complaints were to be processed within forty-eight hours. The city's Department of Urban Renewal would be responsible for reporting cases of discrimination to the Commission on Human Relations, and it would be responsible for assisting families wishing to relocate in any area of the city of Chicago. Discriminatory practices by banking and mortgage institutions would also be carefully monitored, and to facilitate these goals, education and action programmes were to be undertaken by organisations within the city.

King's announcement that the march to Cicero would not take place angered many who had longed for the opportunity to march into Cicero. However, King and others in the SCLC were concerned about how long the movement would be able to sustain the Chicago campaign. For them, the Summit Agreement seemed a sensible conclusion; the march to Cicero could always be done later, should the need arise.

In fact, a march to Cicero did take place, despite King's announcement of the Summit Agreement. Fewer than three hundred demon-strators marched through a rowdy and sometimes violent crowd in Cicero. Local leaders had organised this march and King was not present. Yet the march did prove that Cicero would no longer be able to exclude African-Americans. In itself, the march did little to win any concessions from the Chicago officials, but for many, it was a great psychological victory. Perhaps most poignant of all was the visible social change that had taken place in Chicago. Real-estate agents had been forced to change their segregation practices: property in formerly all-white areas was offered to African-American families. However, many of these families now needed to increase their income in order to afford these properties. It was a need that would be addressed vigorously.

Memphis and the Promised Land

We as a people will get to the promised land.

King had become increasingly vocal in his opposition to the Vietnam War. In April 1967 he called for the Johnson administration to adopt a five-point plan in order to end the war. This plan included an end to all bombing, the declaration of a unilateral ceasefire to prepare for negotiation, an end to military build-ups in Southeast Asia to avoid situations similar to that of Vietnam, a realistic acceptance of the National Liberation Front, and a definite date by which all foreign troops were to be withdrawn from Vietnam, in accordance with the 1954 Geneva Agreement. He extended his appeal to the whole nation when he announced the reasons for his opposition to the American war in Vietnam and his five point programme for peace.

King's reasons for opposing the war were that failure to reach a negotiated settlement would result in Chinese involvement in the war and possibly a world war. His opposition was also influenced by his non-violent stand throughout the civil rights struggle; to do otherwise would be inconsistent with his life's work.

In Memphis, Tennessee, the need for economic enfranchisement was becoming an important issue. King's view was that the solution to the poverty question lay with a guaranteed annual income.

The national undertaking of Operation Breadbasket was to assign commerce and industry the major role of creating opportunities for the hiring of the economically disadvantaged. King, however, also encouraged African-Americans to organise themselves into unions when they found themselves in the lowest paid jobs, so as to enable them to enter into collective bargaining with their employers. He was increasingly conscious that the reformation of the institutions of American society was not enough to bring about the changes that the movement sought. The victory in Montgomery, the experiences in Albany and the great gains won in Birmingham and Selma clearly indicated to King that America needed to be reconstructed. It would mean the nationalisation of major industries but also a revolution in the thinking of every American citizen. A new kind of American with reformed values was needed.

Experiences in the Chicago campaign had forced King to re-examine the nonviolent position he had taken; the SNCC's new militancy continually questioned his tactics, and King, in turn, was becoming more critical of the federal government as he became increasingly alarmed at the connection between the evil of racism, economic exploitation and militarism. Despite this, Carl Stokes stood for mayor in Cleveland, Ohio, in 1967. He won the Democratic primary election and went on to become mayor of Cleveland. No major American city had ever before elected an African-American mayor.

Twelve months later, in October, at the Olympic games in Mexico, Tommie Smith and John Carlos stood with their clenched fists raised in black gloves - the black power salute - after they received their respective gold and bronze medals in the men's 200 m finals. This was 1968 and America was changing. However, nonviolent protests were still being planned. These plans were to disrupt Washington, DC, to engender the social change that would force the Johnson administration to review its foreign and domestic policies. This would be one of King's last major demonstrations. It was a last desperate attempt to induce America to embrace the nonviolent approach to social change. It was to be called the Poor People's Campaign.

The timetable for this was to commence in April 1968. It would attempt to foster changes throughout America: the political integration of African-Americans into mainstream American society. It would involve volunteers from Mississippi, Boston, Chicago and Virginia, who would journey to Washington where they would sally daily to the Senate, the House of Representatives and Cabinet departments such as Health, Education, and Welfare. The central demand was for a $12 billion bill of rights. This would assist in the guaranteeing of employment for those able to work but unemployed, provide income for those unable to work, end housing discrimination, and enforce racially integrated education. The need had already been highlighted in the riots of 1967 in Detroit, Michigan, and these needs had been further recognised by the National Advisory Commission on Civil Disorders. Its report concluded that America was "moving towards two societies, one black, one white - separate and unequal." It recommended sweeping programmes in housing, job creation, education and welfare.

However, these plans for a march on Washington would be delayed somewhat by a major incident on 4 April 1968.

Meanwhile, in Memphis, Tennessee, a strike by African-American sanitation workers begun on

12 February, 1968 had drawn King's attention. The mayor of Memphis, Henry Loeb, refused to recognise the strikers' union and the grievance that there had been racial discrimination in the continued hiring of white workers while African-American workers were sent home without pay. King was asked to help. He addressed an audience at the Mason Temple in that month of March. He would return again in April.

Even before his return to Memphis to support the sanitation workers' strike, scheduled for 5 April, King had received threats against his life. On arrival in Memphis, King and other members of the SCLC checked into the Lorraine Motel.

The sanitation workers' march in Memphis was banned by a federal court injunction because a previous demonstration had ended with the police shooting a sixteen-year-old boy. King, however, was determined that the march would go ahead. He was in defiant mood: "We stand by the First Amendment," he stated.

On Wednesday, 3 April, King sent Ralph Abernathy to convey his apologies to the congregation at the Mason Temple that rainy night, as he did not expect to attend. However, he changed his mind when Abernathy telephoned to say that the crowd insisted on his presence. When he arrived he spoke to them:

I left Atlanta this morning . . . And then I got into Memphis. And some began to say . . . what would happen to me from some of our sick white brothers. . . . But it doesn't matter with me now. Because I've been to the mountaintop. . . . And I've looked over. And I've seen the promised land. I may not get there with you. But I want you to know tonight, that we, as a people will get to the promised land. . . . I'm not worried about anything. I'm not fearing any man. Mine eyes have seen the glory of the coming of the Lord.

This was King's last public address. The next day, shortly after 6 p.m., he was shot and killed on the balcony of the Lorraine Motel. This was 4 April 1968, Memphis.

Time Marches On

King's assassination did not halt the plans to march on Washington. The Poor people's Campaign - to march from Marks, Mississippi to Washington, DC, and camp outside the government offices until their demands were met - still went ahead. They marched to Washington, set up camp, and named it Resurrection City. In the coming months the rain fell and Washington officials ensured that the demonstrators were removed and Resurrection City was destroyed.

The SCLC had benefited greatly from the TV news coverage that broadcast images of the African-Americans' plight. It now seemed as though the movement had ended. In fact, the movement had taken a new direction. The nonviolent approach had already instilled a great sense of pride and dignity among African-Americans. This pride and dignity were most eloquently expressed in the coming years.

In 1972, Gary, Indiana, was the venue for the

meeting of African-American nationalists and elected officials. It was a demonstration of the great spirit that thrived despite the ending of the epic era of the civil rights movement under the leadership of Martin Luther King, Jr., and the SCLC. In this year, in the month of March, some eight thousand people gathered to agree on a national agenda for African-Americans.

Jesse Jackson articulated the mood and tone of that convention when he said that African-Americans represented some twenty-five million of the US population and that "the water has broken, the blood has spilled, a new black baby is going to be born." Thus, Jackson referred to the birth of a new African-American nation in America that reflected a new appreciation of itself.

Since 1955, African-Americans had challenged and changed America in a way that they had never done before. However, it was the 1963 march on Washington that would remain in the minds of millions as the example of black

America capturing the attention of all the world. Commemorative marches would follow to mark the magnificence of this march. One of the most significant of these was the 1993 Anniversary March. This was special because it marked thirty years since King's 'I have a dream' speech. It allowed one to measure the advancement of the struggle since King's death.

In those thirty years, the movement had changed. It had lost its sweeping momentum to instigate social reforms and policies, and many now argued that the gains won in its civil rights years were lost in the following decades of the 1970s and 1980s. To these people, the 1963 march on Washington was the high point of the civil rights movement.

The thirtieth anniversary march on Washington was scheduled for Saturday, 28 August 1993. It would represent the passing of the torch of the struggle to the younger generation. The theme for this march was jobs, justice and peace. That the march should take place, however, underlined the fact that 'the dream' of 1963 had not been completely realised. Yet, as with all dreams, it presented a vision of an alternative way of life.

Joseph Lowery, head of the SCLC, saw the anniversary march as an opportunity to make that dream a reality through the hard work of the Coalition of Conscience. This coalition represented some two hundred civil and human rights, religious, labour and peace organisations. Solidarity was seen as the key to tapping the nation's great wealth of opportunities and investment in all America's people.

Walter Fonteroy had the task of organising this march - he had already played a role in the 1963 march. However, the demands of 1993 were more varied than the united call for justice and freedom in 1963; then, King mobilised 250,000 people to let the nation and the world know that African-Americans were tired of the segregation and racial discrimination that had excluded them from the mainstream of American society.

The march in 1993 was not organised by the African-American civil rights groups alone, nor was it for the concerns of African-Americans alone. This time the participants would march under many banners, and the SCLC allied itself with the Coalition of Conscience. The issues did not rest upon the unquestionable right to freedom and justice, as they did in 1963. At the 1963 march, Martin Luther King, Jr., and the civil rights movement challenged America to be what it ought to be.

As in 1963, there was some reliance on the federal government. This time the agenda was quite elaborate. Legislation was outlined and the message was to "contact your Senators and Representatives and urge them to support the critical legislation." Among the demands for jobs was the Local Partnership Act of 1993. This bill authorised $3 billion in payments to units of local government, for the years 1993 and 1994 to develop a revenue-sharing programme to allow local governments to rehire unemployed workers or develop programmes in education, health and social services.

However, it is on the question of freedom that King's stirring oratory is best remembered. This was the theme that brought together the quarter of a million gathered crowd at the Lincoln Memorial in 1963. They were gathered to let Congress know the magnitude of the injustice being perpetrated: in particular, on the matter of voting rights. They were not a mob; they were disciplined demonstrators, and their large numbers could easily have brought Washington to a crippling standstill. President Kennedy knew this and his efforts to assist in the finances of the march were in some ways a recognition of this fact and also an attempt to keep open a window of opportunity for dialogue and discussion.

Discussions on civil rights did take place after the march with President Kennedy. This was in contrast to 1993 when President Bill Clinton decided that he would rather holiday in Martha's Vineyard, Massachusetts. In response to this, Joseph Lowery of the SCLC commented that there is a vineyard in the neighbourhoods of the African-American communities, while Ben Chavius of the NAACP pointedly stated that President Clinton should not forget the communities that had elected him.

Yet King's reference point in 1963 for justice went back to 1776, the year of the Declaration of Independence. This was the beginning of America's constitutional history when she claimed the right to govern herself henceforth.

We hold these truths to be self-evident, that all men are created equal, that they are endowed by their Creator with certain unalienable rights, that among these are life, liberty, and the pursuit of happiness.

It was with particular reference to these words of Thomas Jefferson that the civil rights movement challenged America: "We hold these truths to be self-evident that all men are created equal." Yet the movement had proved that there was nothing "self-evident" about racial equality in America; it was only clear that there were two societies in America, black and white, separate and unequal. With this reference, King challenged America to "live out the true meaning of its creed, 'We hold these truths to be self-evident that all men are created equal.'" At this point, it was felt that the movement could shame the nation and force a change of heart, but racial segregation knew no shame and had no conscience.

In 1993 the thirtieth-anniversary march was focused on jobs, justice and peace. The peace aspect of this demonstration was central. It was only through peace that one could constructively contemplate other ways of life that bring freedom and happiness.

The younger speakers at the march emphasised the need for "peace in the neighbourhood". This call to end the violence and murder in the neighbourhoods of America was a response to an issue that had become an increasing concern for many Americans in the early 1990s. In August 1993, some 6,000 people in the USA were killed in drug-related violence. Yet it was Jesse Jackson who mentioned that in Los Angeles in May 1992 an African-American man, Rodney King, became instantly known when his beating by white Los Angeles police officers was filmed for all the world to see. The beating enraged the African-American community of Los Angeles, and the acquittal of the four policemen responsible set Los Angeles ablaze with rioting that was compared to the Watts riots in 1965. Watts had underlined the need for the National Advisory Commission on Civil Disorders. The riots in 1993 following the beating saw President Bush call in the military.

In 1963 the question of peace was not so central to the theme of the demonstrators. The Vietnam war issue had not gripped America in the way it would later between 1965 and 1974. Some 275,000 African-Americans would serve in the armed forces in Vietnam; more than 5500 would die in combat. This reality lay ahead for America.

There were concerted attempts to stress global

peace at the 1993 march.The coalition in its listed demands urged people to support legislation to establish an enterprise fund for a democratic South Africa.This fund was to provide shared investments, grants, loans, feasibility studies as well as education and training to enable the indigenous South Africans to participate effectively in the economic development of post- apartheid South Africa. This was effectively a call for private and public sources to be developed in that country so as to enhance economic development for the benefit of those disadvantaged by the apartheid system. The plan would help to shape the new South Africa.

In the 1993 march on Washington, there was no mention of the Star Wars programme, introduced in 1983 by President Ronald Reagan. This plan, to build a space shield of lasers and neutron beams, cost America $3 billion in 1993. The programme of Star Wars would ensure that in the event of any nuclear attack, zigmos would destroy incoming nuclear missiles before they reached the USA. This would allow the USA to launch a retaliatory strike without the fear of a succeeding attack. Congress's approval of this billion-dollar project showed that warfare had become extremely sophisticated in America of the 1980s, compared to 1965 and the battlefields of Vietnam. By 1993, many, including Joseph Lowery of the SCLC, thought that a radical reduction in military spending and production was needed.

It was, however, the call for justice that enabled one most clearly to see the continuity between the 1963 march and the 1993 march. In 1963 African-Americans had marched on Washington in order to cash a cheque that would give them upon demand "the riches of freedom and the security of justice," as King expressed it. America could no longer resist this argument: freedom and justice had been a part of the American Constitution for generations, and yet it had not been implemented in any true and meaningful way. America had to change.

In 1993, justice meant effective policies and

resource allocation, to aid the people, communities and environments in most need of attention. This concept of justice included race, gender, age, sexual orientation, mental and physical disabilities and issues of religion and poverty. Many of these issues required the bringing of pressure to bear on the federal government. This meant that in 1993 the coalition was calling for support for a bill to set up a programme to ensure compliance with all environmental, health and safety laws with emphasis on equal protection of public health. There was, for instance, support for a bill to combat violence and crimes against women.

There was support for a bill which brought a united call from all parties in the coalition. The establishment of a Martin Luther King Day had already been conceded in 1983 - to come into effect in 1986 as an official national holiday. However, the coalition call to support the King National Holiday and Service Bill also asked for a National Service Day to promote community service.

Despite this reliance on the federal government to instigate changes, the coalition did not consider itself subject to any of the political parties. Joseph Lowery and the SCLC saw the need for "permanent political principles" as opposed to "permanent political party loyalties". There was also concern that if the political parties did not meet the principles of the coalition, the coalition would present candidates independent of the main political parties.

The question of unity was still an important factor in the success of the SCLC and the continuing struggle for equality and a better life. In 1993 as in 1972, the matter remained paramount in all efforts for social change, as epitomised by Mayor Richard Hatcher of Gary, Indiana at the National Black Political Convention:

> Will we walk in unity or disperse in one thousand different directions . . . will we do what must be done? These are the questions confronting us . . . and you and I are the only ones that can answer them, and history will be the judge.

Selected Bibliography

Books and Pamphlets

Branch, Taylor. 1990. *Parting the Waters: Martin Luther King and the Civil Rights Movement 1954-1963.* London, PaperMac.

Clarke, John Henrik. 1995. *Who Betrayed the African World Revolution? and Other Speeches.* New York, Third World Press.

Garrow, David. 1993. *Baring the Cross: Martin Luther King, Jr. and the Southern Christian Leadership Conference.* London, Vintage.

Grimshaw, Anna (ed.). 1993. *The CLR James Reader.* Oxford, Blackwell Publishers.

Hitchings, Thomas, E. (et al. ed.). 1993. *Facts on File Yearbook.* New York, Facts on File, Inc.

____. (et al ed.). 1968. *Indexed Record of World Events.* New York, Facts on File.

King Jr., Martin Luther. 1958. *Stride Toward Freedom: The Montgomery Story.* New York, Harper and Row.

____. 1963. *Strength to Love.* New York, Harper and Row.

____. 1964. *Why We Can't Wait.* New York, Mentor.

____. 1967. *Where Do We Go from Here? Chaos or*

Community. New York, Harper and Row.1968.

___. *The Trumpet of Conscience.* New York, Harper and Row.

Lewis, David. 1970. *Martin Luther King: A Critical Biography.* London, Allen Lane and The Penguin Press.

Oates, Stephen B. 1982. *Let the Trumpet Sound: The Life of Martin Luther King, Jr.* London, Search Press.

Rothman, John. (et al. ed.). 1969. *New York Times Index.* New York, Arno Press.

Shawki, Ahmed (ed.). 1990. *International Socialism (47).* London, International Socialism.

Shuker, Nancy. 1985. *Martin Luther King.* New York, Chelsea House Publishers

Sobel, Lester (et al ed.). 1969 *Facts on File Yearbook.* New York, Facts on File.

The King Center (Atlanta, Georgia)

Box 1, File 5, MIA Affiliations.

Box 4, File 31, Birmingham Jail Letters, May - August 1963.

____, File 32, Black Power Conference, October 1966.

Box 9, File 13, *Ebony*.

Box 15, File 16, Malcolm X, March 1964 - February 1965.

Box 120, File 8, Emancipation Document to President John F. Kennedy

____, File 15, Press Release on Burned Churches in 1963.

____ File 17, Press Release on Birmingham Jailed Students.

Box 122, File 3, Press Release on Plans for Selma.

Box 122, File 15, Press Release on Resolution of Vietnam War.

____, File 17, Manifesto of Meredith March.

Box 123, File 15, Organisation of March on Washington.

____, File 20, Operation Breadbasket 1964.

Meetings

Bruce Keyes (The King Center) - August 1993.

John Lewis (former president of SNCC) - August 1993

Rev. Osburn (SCLC) - August 1993.

INDEX

Buy the book at your local bookstore or use this convenient coupon for ordering.

Afrikan Kin Publications
P.O.Box 4211
London
SE14 6LP

Please send me _____ * copy/copies of 'The Life and Death of Martin Luther King'.

I am enclosing * US$ _____/£___. (Please add US$3.50 or £2.50 for P&P).

I am sending a * cheque / money order and I realise that prices and numbers are subject to change without notice.
PRINT
Name:

Address:

Allow 28 days for delivery

This offer is subject to withdrawal without notice.

*= delete as appropriate